Original title:
Lemonade Days

Copyright © 2025 Creative Arts Management OÜ
All rights reserved.

Author: Elias Marchant
ISBN HARDBACK: 978-1-80586-273-4
ISBN PAPERBACK: 978-1-80586-745-6

Citrus Kisses

A splash of yellow, oh so bright,
In glasses tall, what a sight!
Sips of sunshine, laughter rings,
Each sip a dance, the joy it brings.

Sticky fingers, a tart delight,
Pucker up, we giggle light.
Juggling cups, we spill a bit,
But that's just part of the fun, admit!

Radiant Refreshment

Sunshine in a cup, we cheer,
With flavors bold, it's almost sheer!
A twist of lime, a silly face,
We sip and grin in our bright place.

Dancing ants come join our spree,
While sugar sticks like honeybee.
We laugh until our tummies ache,
While dreaming sweet of frosty lakes.

Sweetness from Nature

Nature's gift in shades of gold,
Quenching thirst, a tale retold.
Pitted fruit and zesty zest,
Brings out the giggles at our best.

A picnic blanket, spills and laughs,
Counting sips while dodging shafts.
Those dribbles down our chins and cheeks,
Become the laughter, funny peaks.

Pink-Tinged Memories

A pitcher full of rosy bliss,
Stir in the fun, don't you miss!
Colorful straws like rainbow dreams,
We sip in sync with silly beams.

Chasing each other, cups in hand,
Running wild across the land.
Each gulp a memory, fresh and pure,
Creating smiles that will endure!

When Life Gives You Citrus

When life hands you fruit, don't fret,
Just grab a shaker and don't you sweat.
Squeeze out the zest, let laughter flow,
Add sugar, water, and let's steal the show.

Make a silly face, and twirl the cup,
With splashes of joy, we'll drink it up.
Life's sour notes can't hold us down,
With a twist and a grin, we'll wear the crown.

Pitcher of Possibilities

In a pitcher, dreams swirl like a dance,
Tigger's leap is not just for chance.
Pour in the giggles, add splashes of fun,
Mixing our quirks 'til the day is done.

Each ice cube clinks, a jolly refrain,
Funny little thoughts, like drops of rain.
Sipping on sunshine with sprigs of cheer,
Stirring up joy, oh how we steer!

Sun-filled Reflections

Golden rays bounce in a twisty glass,
Sunshine smiles like a playful class.
With every sip, the giggles ignite,
Bubbles of joy in the warm twilight.

A reflection of laughter, a splash of wit,
Let's savor the moments; let's not quit.
Under blue skies, we'll dance and play,
With every burst, we'll chase blues away.

Breezy Days and Sweet Rays

Breezy days call for a chilled delight,
Citrus whispers in the soft sunlight.
Sipping slow with friends by my side,
In this funny world, let's take a ride.

Catch the laughter like a breeze in spring,
Bright yellow faces, joy on a string.
With every giggle that jumps our way,
We'll toast to the sweetness, come what may.

A Sip of Radiance

In the sun, we laugh and play,
Sipping drinks that shine like day.
Yellow cups in hand we share,
Tasting joy—it fills the air.

Giggling as the ice cubes clink,
Straws like rockets, quick in sync.
Sticky fingers, smiles abound,
A splash of fun, we're joy unbound.

Chasing shadows, racing fast,
Every sip, a spell is cast.
With every twist, a zesty cheer,
We sip our joy, we hold it dear.

Blissful Quench

Fizzy bubbles tickle noses,
Squeezing out what summer poses.
A splash of glee in sunny cups,
Swirling flavors, all hiccups.

Runny jokes and silly puns,
Underneath the bright warm suns.
Chasing laughter with a gulp,
Tooul in a happy, fizzy pulp.

Straw hats flying, feet in sand,
With every sip, we make a stand.
Giggles burst like citrus zest,
In this bliss, we are the best.

Garden of Citrus

In a garden full of cheer,
Colors dancing, bright and near.
Lemon trees with laughter grow,
Sipping sunshine, let it flow.

Frolicking like bees in bloom,
Honeyed words in every room.
With each twist, a story spins,
Citrus smiles, where joy begins.

Buzzing bees with happy hearts,
Nature's art in tangy parts.
Stirring dreams with every sip,
In this garden, we take a trip.

The Flavor of Youth

Bicycle rides in golden glow,
Kicks up dust wherever we go.
Sweet citrus smiles, bold and bright,
In every cup, pure delight.

Chasing tales of summers past,
Witty quips and friendships cast.
With fizzy drinks in frosty hands,
We dance through life, make our plans.

Carefree days, a joyful rush,
Like lemonade's sweet, zesty hush.
With every sip, we raise our cheer,
For in our hearts, youth lingers near.

Breezy Overtones

Under the sun, we laugh and play,
Sipping sweet drinks, bright as the day,
Sticky fingers, a joyful crew,
Chasing our dreams, just me and you.

With hats that blow when the wind kicks in,
We dance and twirl, let the fun begin,
The sky's a stage, the clouds our friends,
Our giggles echo, the joy never ends.

Catching Sunbeams

In a jar we catch the golden glow,
Wonders of summer in a vibrant flow,
Silly plans wrapped in laughter's embrace,
A splash of mischief, a dash of grace.

We stumble and trip on the sunny trails,
Sharing wild tales where friendship prevails,
With juice-stained lips and hearts so free,
We toast to the moments just you and me.

The Color of Happiness

Bright hues splash like a painter's brush,
In every sip, we feel the rush,
Giggles erupt from the silliest fights,
As we chase the shadows and play with lights.

Smiles like rainbows, so big and wide,
Citrus flavors that we can't hide,
With each little sip, a new tale spins,
In this vibrant world, the laughter begins.

Ribbons of Citrus Light

A twist of the wrist, a shake, and a grin,
The splash of a smile as the fun times begin,
We dance through the haze of a sun-kissed day,
With every sweet sip, the worries decay.

Curly straws make silly drinks rise high,
We sip and we slurp, oh me, oh my!
Each round of laughter wraps us so tight,
In this zesty world, everything feels right.

A Garden of Refreshments

In a patch of bright sunshine,
Where fruits gather and smile,
The zesty lemon laughs out loud,
As squirrels dance in style.

A jug spills joy and giggles,
Each sip a splash of cheer,
Even the ants start to wobble,
Their tiny feet full of beer.

Straw hats tilt with flair,
While grasshoppers play a tune,
The butterflies giggle softly,
And dance beneath the moon.

A picnic blanket shimmers,
With snacks all over the place,
As spritzers tickle our noses,
We toast to silliness in space.

Spritz of Brilliance

A twist of bright yellow, oh what a sight,
As bubbles pop with delight in the air,
The world feels lighter, so merry and bright,
Inviting the clouds to join in our flair.

Sip after sip, the giggles explode,
While lemonade rainbows splash in the breeze,
The sun wears sunglasses to lighten the load,
As bees throw a party atop all the trees.

Each gulp brings cheer, like a ticklish breeze,
We sway with the flowers, as joy spirals high,
With citrus confetti filling our knees,
In this garden of laughter, we all fly.

The world tops off with a spritz and a smile,
Funny faces made from fruity delight,
In this land of refreshment, stay for a while,
And relish the laughter beneath warmth's invite.

Sweet Citrus Whispers

Under a canopy of sparkling fruit,
Whispers of sweetness brush past the ear.
We sip on the sunshine, the taste so astute,
And giggles erupt when things get unclear.

Naps taken short, on the grass all around,
With halos of lemon perched on our heads,
Chasing our shadows, we run with no sound,
In a citrusy world, the laughter spreads.

Twirling the straws, we dance in a line,
Bubbly concoctions elevate mood,
With each little slurp, we're feeling divine,
A ruckus of joy in sweet brotherhood.

Bright days drip down like a colorful paint,
We splash in the moments, no reason to wait,
With smiles as wide as a lemon we paint,
Crafting our stories, it's never too late.

Bracing Under the Sun

A taste of tangy, a splash of zest,
In the heart of a summer so golden and bright,
We chase after laughter, it's simply the best,
With cups raised high, we toast to our plight.

The children are giggling, the adults unwind,
While ice cubes cling to their frosted glasses,
Each moment delicious, like dreams intertwined,
As the sun plays peekaboo through green grasses.

Splashes of sweetness, a citrusy cheer,
We bubble like soda, a fizzy delight,
The air is alive, no worries or fear,
In the glow of the dusk, everything feels right.

Let's savor this mischief, let joy overflow,
For beneath this bright sun, our spirits all soar,
With each drop that dances, we paint tales aglow,
In this realm of refreshment, who could want more?

Refreshing Whispers

On a sunny patch where giggles bloom,
Sipping citrus dreams, we chase the gloom.
Sticky fingers wave like flapping wings,
As we frolic, laughter forever sings.

Bubbles pop like fireflies in flight,
Gulping joy beneath the cool twilight.
A splash of zest from our silly smiles,
We dance in puddles, running for miles.

The Taste of Summer

Sour and sweet, a frosty treat,
Tangy notes drumming to our beat.
Lemon peels in wild forms of art,
We serve the world with a zesty heart.

Ice cubes jingle like a merry band,
We toast to mischief with wobbling hands.
Sunshine becomes our vibrant friend,
With every sip, we joyfully blend.

Yellow Hues and Echoes

Golden rays painted on our skin,
We dive into flavors, let the fun begin.
In a pitcher filled with giggles and cheer,
We sip from cups overflowing with cheer.

Every drop whispers secrets of joy,
As we twirl and laugh, playful and coy.
The tartness tangles, a game we play,
With every sip, we chase blues away.

A Glass Half Full

Half full of hope, half full of fun,
Under the sun, we jitter and run.
With every gulp, our worries fade,
Each twist of fate, a lemon parade.

A toast to the silly, the sweet and the sour,
We squeeze out laughter, our finest hour.
Sloshing about in a fruity spree,
In this zesty world, we're wild and free.

Playful Refreshments

In the sun, we take a sip,
Sweet and tangy, on our lips.
Laughter bubbles, bright and clear,
Cheers to summer, oh so near!

Beneath the tree, a picnic spread,
Jokes fly by, and laughter's bred.
Sparkling drinks in tiny cups,
Joy just beams, it never ups!

A splash of joy, a twist of zest,
Warm days call for our very best.
Friends gather round, with smiles so wide,
This playful moment, a joyful ride.

So pour another, let's share a cheer,
With every sip, the fun draws near.
Beneath the rays, we drink and play,
In every drop, we find our way!

A Tapestry of Citrus

Bright and yellow, on the stand,
Citrus treasures, oh so grand.
Each slice spins a tale so sweet,
In this feast, we dance on feet.

Zesty notes and giggles blend,
Every sip's a playful trend.
Sour face or joyful grin,
Life's a joke, and we all win!

Under twinkling skies we meet,
Chasing dreams with tangy treat.
A swirl of colors, bright and bold,
Every moment feels like gold.

Neighbors join, the fun's in play,
We sip and spill the time away.
Juicy tales and laughter flows,
In our patch, the sunlight glows!

The Last Squeeze

Clouds of laughter fill the air,
As we gather without a care.
The pitcher's empty, not a drop,
But still our giggles never stop.

In the yard, we toss our woes,
Squeezing life from every pose.
Mischief dances on the grass,
Sours and sweets, we raise a glass.

Sunshine drips from leafy trees,
A playful breeze whispers with ease.
We'll toast to smiles that linger long,
Our hearts in sync, a merry song.

So when the fun begins to wane,
We'll squeeze more joy from every grain.
With memories fresh from citrus cheer,
We'll laugh and cherish the time here!

Cool Comforts

Ice cubes clink in summer's heat,
Tasting joy with every treat.
Brightly colored, drinks on hand,
We create our own wonderland.

Splashing laughter, droplets ring,
As we dance, and sunlight sings.
With every gulp, the smiles grow,
Cooling winds, we gently flow.

Under shades of leafy green,
We share secrets, none unseen.
Fizzy bubbles, sparkling streams,
In our cups, we mix our dreams.

So raise a toast, let spirits shine,
Refreshment's here, and all is fine.
In the warmth, we find our place,
With silly moments we embrace!

Tart Temptations

Sipping sunshine from a jar,
Laughs bubble as we spar.
Sweet and sour, what a mix,
Life's a game of citrus tricks.

Ice cubes clink in joyful dance,
A splash, a glug, a silly chance.
Giggling while we spill and slosh,
In this fruity, fizzy posh.

Lemon hats upon our heads,
Juicy puddles where we tread.
Watch those wrinkled faces frown,
As we knock each other down.

With each sip, the laughter flows,
Chasing curls and sunny shows.
Crazy fun, we live today,
In our tart, zesty play.

Picnic Pleasures

Blankets spread on grassy grounds,
Pies and snacks—the best of sounds.
Tasting tang in every sip,
As we giggle and we trip.

Ants march as if they own the feast,
While we joke, laughter unleashed.
Cups in hand, we toast so high,
Squirrels jeer, the birds fly by.

Splashing drops on noses round,
Funny faces all abound.
Chasing bubbles, we collide,
In our bubbly, joyous ride.

Wobbly cakes and squeezy straws,
Wrapped in laughter and applause.
Picnics burst with silly cheer,
Where every sip brings friends near.

The Art of Flavor

Whirl and twirl the zesty blend,
Mismatched flavors, what a trend!
Smiles served on iced trays right,
Sipping joy, a pure delight.

Taste explosion with a twist,
Sour giggles, can't resist.
Sticky fingers, fruit adorned,
In this fun, we're all reborn.

Painted cups like work of art,
Fruity vibes that warm the heart.
Stirring up the laughter loud,
In our zesty, crazy crowd.

Let's exchange comedic bets,
Who can sip without regrets?
With each slurp — a tale to tell,
In this art, we laugh so well.

Summery Elixirs

Fizzy dreams in every glass,
Daring friends to take a pass.
Bubbles form a giggly show,
Taking sips, we steal the glow.

Slipping splashes all around,
Chasing giggles, joy unbound.
Zingy elixirs, tastes collide,
On this sunny, thrill-filled ride.

Catch a cloud or let it go,
Friends in chaos steal the show.
Sloppy sips, and sticky grins,
In this madness, everyone wins.

Sunset hues, the day now fades,
Laughter lingers in cascades.
Raise your cup, let's make a toast,
To summer fun, we love the most!

Sweet and Tangy Journeys

A zesty quest from sun to shore,
With cups in hand, we sing and roar.
Sour escapades made sweet with cheer,
Laughter bubbling up, oh so near.

We frolic through the citrus trees,
Catching sunlight, dancing with ease.
Faces puckered, but smiles ignite,
This jovial ride feels just right.

Jars of joy on the kitchen shelf,
We sip and giggle, just like ourselves.
A splash of fun in every drink,
Brightened moments make hearts rethink.

Adventure calls in every drop,
Sipping fun till we all plop.
Memory's tartness in the air,
Happiness brews, a perfect share.

Radiance in Every Sip

Bright sunshine winked in every glass,
Giddy moments fly by like grass.
Fizzy thrills and playful blends,
As giggles dance, the fun transcends.

We gather round with thoughts so spry,
Tickled pink by the sweet supply.
Sips that sparkle, tickling the tongue,
As laughter lingers and songs are sung.

Colors swirl like a joyful kite,
Chasing shadows from day to night.
Citrusy splashes make hearts ignite,
Radiant memories shining bright.

Every time we clink our cups,
Joy cascades; we lift our ups.
A sugary tingle, life's delight,
In every sip, we unite tonight.

A Symphony of Flavors

Notes of tang in harmony play,
Whispers of fruit in a bright ballet.
Each sip a joyful little tune,
Sipping sunshine, morning to noon.

The pitter-patter of drops so sweet,
Bringing together life's little treats.
Flavorful laughter fills the air,
The zest of life we boldly share.

Cupfuls of cheer on a playful breeze,
Each sip tickles, putting minds at ease.
Curious blends with a splash of fun,
A tune of happiness everyone.

In this glass, a party's begun,
Hilarity flows with each little pun.
Savoring moments that feel like art,
A symphony of flavors warms the heart.

Nostalgic Brews of Brightness

Backyard fun in sunny delight,
Sipping back to days so bright.
Little giggles through the yard,
Life's simple pleasures aren't that hard.

A twist of fruit, a dash of zest,
Chasing friendship, we're both blessed.
Simple joys in absent hues,
Memories ripe with sips and views.

Sour pouts turn to laughter's song,
In breezy afternoons, we belong.
Carefree moments, bright and bold,
Precious elixirs never get old.

Glasses raised to times anew,
With every drop, we feel the hue.
Nostalgic brews of laughter's spark,
Lighting up echoes, bright in the park.

Zesty Memories

We squeezed the fruit in summer's light,
The juice ran wild, an orange fight.
With laughter loud, we spilled it all,
And giggled as it made us fall.

We danced around, our cups held high,
With sticky hands, we waved goodbye.
Each sip a burst, each grin a prize,
As bright as sun in azure skies.

The nightime brought a zesty cheer,
As fireflies twinkled, drawing near.
We sipped and sang with zestful dreams,
Glow of our joy, or so it seems.

In every gulp, a chuckle flies,
As laughter sparkles, never lies.
Together we found sweet delight,
In sunny tales long past the night.

Sun-Kissed Sips

On porch we lounged, the drinks were cold,
A kingdom made of tales retold.
With lemon rings and minty swirls,
Our cups were crowns, oh how they twirl!

The dog chased shadows, tripped on toes,
While giggles burst like poppy blooms.
A splash, a squirt, a citrus fight,
Our sips transformed the day to night.

With cheerful sips of tart and sweet,
We conquered summers, never beat.
Each glass we raised, a toast to glow,
Cheers to the smiles that overflow!

In every drop, a joke held tight,
With every laugh, we took our flight.
The sun kissed us with golden rays,
Forever bound in sun-kissed days.

Citrus Reverie

In gardens grand, we'd hunt for treats,
Beneath the trees, a world of feats.
A splash of juice, a classic blend,
With every sip, our spirits mend.

The cat would jump, the kids would scream,
As lemonade cascaded like a dream.
We clinked our cups with glee and cheer,
As summer's warmth drew ever near.

With zest and smiles, we spun around,
Our laughter echoed, joy unbound.
A sip of sunshine in our hands,
When life was made of glowing strands.

In citrus worlds where fun's the guide,
Each moment cherished, side by side.
We'll toast the past with glowing eyes,
In citrus dreams where laughter flies.

Sweetened Sunshine

With sugar spills and giggles grand,
We never knew how fast it'd land.
In cups of joy, we'd raise our cheers,
To every hope that appears through tears.

The blender whirred, the ice did crash,
As kids all played with silly splash.
Bright colored straws like candy lanes,
Each sip a burst, a sweet refrain.

From sunlit morn to starlit night,
We danced around in pure delight.
Each glass a trophy, laughter found,
In sticky hands, our joy unbound.

With smiles as bright as summer's glow,
We'll treasure this sweet afterglow.
As memories sweeten every way,
In sunshine's warmth, we choose to stay.

Golden Drops of Bliss

A glass in hand, I grin wide,
The sun shines bright, I take a ride.
Sipping sweet, with straw in place,
Laughter dances, what a taste!

Friends all gather, jokes take flight,
Spilling tales under sunlight.
Fumbling ice, a splash or two,
Sticky fingers, laughter grew!

Sour moments tossed away,
Sugar drops at the play.
Life's a treat, let's raise a toast,
To frothy joys we love the most!

Waves of flavor, zest so bold,
In every gulp, new stories told.
Golden magic in a glass,
These sunny days should always last!

Frosted Memories

Chillin' out with friends so dear,
Sipping sparkly drinks, full of cheer.
Frosty cups, they slip and slide,
Giggles echo, can't hide the pride!

Sticky fun, we spill and laugh,
Tart and sweet, a perfect craft.
Splashes from a frosty glass,
Whirlin' wonder, time will pass!

Colorful straws that twist and bend,
Memories made that won't soon end.
Droplets drip like silly streams,
Floating on our summer dreams!

Breezy air and cheerful song,
Join the fun; it won't be long.
Frosted joy, a blissful ride,
Join the laughter, there's room inside!

Days of Citrus Bliss

Sun-kissed mornings, joy's display,
Citrus zest makes worries sway.
Twisting limes and tangy squeeze,
In this sun, the world's at ease!

Bubbles fizz as laughter sings,
Frolic freely, what joy it brings!
Chasing shadows, bright and sly,
With every sip, we touch the sky!

Mixing flavors, oh what fun,
Chasing rays until we're done.
Moments burst like sunlit rays,
Wasting time in playful haze!

Fruity treats in every blend,
With pals beside, the laughter won't end.
Sloshing drinks and silly cheers,
These sunny days create no fears!

Chill of a Summer Storm

Clouds roll in, but spirits rise,
Sipping sweet with sparkly eyes.
Jokes are flying, no need to frown,
Even storms can't drag us down!

Giggling loud as raindrops plop,
Messy fun, we'll never stop.
Wet and wild, we splash about,
Silly faces, there's no doubt!

Vitamin C in every sip,
Zesty taste, let's take a trip.
Puddle jumping, hearts so light,
Our lemonade keeps us bright!

The chill brings smiles, let's all play,
Dancing shadows, soaking gray.
With every gulp, we laugh and cheer,
Stormy days, bring friends so near!

Chill in a Glass

On a bright and sunny street,
Kids are filling cups with glee.
Lemons dance and take a seat,
Watery wishes, oh so free.

Mint leaves twirl in icy cheer,
Sugar sneaks with every stir.
Giggles float, the taste is near,
Catch the smiles as flavors blur.

A splash of joy from pouts of tart,
Fingers sticky, laughter flows.
Sipping slowly, take your part,
This sweet moment surely glows.

Bees are buzzing, flies will play,
A sticky race against the sun.
Quenching thirsts in silly ways,
Feel the fun, we've just begun.

Summer's Tangy Embrace

Squeeze the fruit and feel the zest,
A summer twist, pure delight.
Glasses clink, we're at our best,
Chasing shadows till the night.

Ice cubes laugh and jump around,
Splashing dance in every sip.
Laughter's music is the sound,
As tangy tales begin to drip.

Friends are gathered, feet in sand,
Dripping colors on our shirts.
Sweetness mingles, hand in hand,
Swirling chaos, lemon flirts.

We raise our cups, a silly toast,
For silly things that make us grin.
With every sip, we love the most,
The carefree world that now begins.

Sweetness on the Tongue

A festival of tiny drops,
Chemistry of sugar and fun.
Zesty giggles never stop,
Beneath the balmy, shining sun.

Squirrels peek from leafy trees,
As we slurp our chilly drink.
Tickled tongues in fresh squeezed breeze,
In the shade, we laugh and stink.

Splashing smiles from tip to chin,
Each sip a burst, a sunlit joke.
Flavor fights begin to spin,
In a world where all's bespoke.

Sip by sip, our dreams will rise,
Juggling joy without a care.
What's better than sweet surprise?
In every glass, a summer fair.

Citron Hues

Golden glimmers on the deck,
Chasing clouds with every twist.
A citrus dream, what the heck?
Joyous moments that can't be missed.

Cups are filled with giggly thrills,
Slush and slosh, the perfect blend.
Sun-kissed laughter over spills,
With every taste, our minds transcend.

Painting towns in sticky hues,
We compose our zestful song.
Frothy bubbles, silly blues,
Where the sweet and tangy belong.

Underneath this summer sky,
We trot along in joyful grace.
Citron dreams make spirits fly,
As we sip at a silly pace.

Frosted Sunshine

Zesty smiles on a summer spree,
Lemon slices dance, wild and free.
Chasing sweetness with every sip,
We tumble and giggle, a joy trip.

Sunshine drips on a fuzzy bee,
Buzzing around, what jubilee!
Hermit crabs wear glasses, so chic,
Sipping from coconuts, oh so unique!

With every gulp, laughter bursts,
Sticky fingers, oh how it hurts!
We slip on ice, land with a thud,
Face first in a puddle of citrus mud!

But who cares if we're messy and loud?
We'll shout to the world, "Look how we're proud!"
Our frosted dreams float in the air,
Living our best, without a single care!

Vibrant Drops

Sipping sunshine from a mason jar,
Bright colors twirl, they spread afar.
A twist of whimsy, tang on the tongue,
With giggles of children, our hearts are young.

Drizzled rainbows on a hot sidewalk,
We race with ice cubes, a slippery walk.
Each splash is a tingling, fizzy delight,
As we leap and dance, oh what a sight!

Mismatched straws and silly hats,
A parade of laughter, who needs more than that?
With playful splashes, we paint the day,
Citrusy giggles, come out and play!

In this zany world, where fun never stops,
We balance on lemons, oh how life hops!
Frosty sprinklers, bright sunny rays,
Keep us spinning in vibrant plays!

Citrus Symphony

Notes of orange swirl in the breeze,
Squeezed together, they dance with ease.
Lemon zest pirouettes, oh what a flair,
While grapefruit giggles, floating in air.

The pitch of laughter rises so high,
As lime winks cheekily, oh my oh my!
In this symphony of shady light,
We frolic and play until the night.

With rhythm of sweetness, we sing a tune,
As berries bounce under the glowing moon.
Melodies of merriment fill the day,
With a strum on sweet limes, we sway, we sway!

A fabulous concert of zesty delight,
As the orchestra of jests plays into the night.
In our fruity arena, we shout and cheer,
For every drop brings joy and good cheer!

Days of Refreshing Whimsy

Whimsical clouds drift on a blue screen,
Lemon peels dangling, a funny routine.
Chasing each other with fruity spritz,
Giggles escape like playful glitz.

Cool breezes whistle, they tickle our ears,
As we craft our wishes through bubbly cheers.
Swirling with colors, we snag a swirl,
Slurping our favorites, watch the chaos unfurl!

With funky hats made of citrus delight,
We dance through the sprinkles, lost in the light.
Why walk straight when you can take a slide?
With every hop, our joy is amplified!

These refreshing hours, a spirited spree,
Where laughter flows, oh can't you see?
In a carnival of flavors, we sway and sway,
In this zany playground, we'll laugh all day!

Honeyed Rays

Golden drops in jars we keep,
Sipping slow, no time for sleep.
Lemon twist with silly grin,
Chasing shadows, let the fun begin.

Sunshine spills like painted art,
Giggling bubbles, every heart.
Sour faces turn to glee,
Join the laughter, wild and free.

Grass stains on our happy feet,
Dancing to the summer beat.
Sweet and tart, a perfect blend,
In this warmth, we all transcend.

Sip it slow, or swig it fast,
Moments brightening as they pass.
In the park or by the shore,
Honeyed rays leave us wanting more.

Bubbles in the Breeze

Floating high, where giggles soar,
Bubbles bounce, and spirits roar.
Swirling joy in sunlit skies,
Catch them quick, they're such a prize.

Fizzy fizz with a splash and pop,
Chasing dreams, we'll never stop.
Sipping sunshine, laughter shared,
In this moment, no one's scared.

Wobbly tables, sipping slow,
Sticky fingers, friends in tow.
Sparkling eyes and silly hats,
Dance like no one cares; how about that?

Once we sip, the world is bright,
Bubbles cheer through day and night.
Floating high with no end in sight,
In this breeze, our hearts take flight.

Joyful Quencher

Chilled to chill, the pitcher sways,
Sweetened hue of sunny days.
Laughter bubbles in the glass,
Cheers to moments that won't pass.

Fruity flavors intertwine,
Sipping slow, we feel divine.
Silly straws in every cup,
Letting loose, we're bubbling up.

Caught in laughter, hearts on fire,
Each sip fuels our wild desire.
Hopscotch games and silly races,
In this joy, we find our places.

Time slips by like slipping ice,
In this bliss, we pay no price.
We'll dance our way through every song,
With joy inside, we can't go wrong.

Citrus Sunsets

Evening glow with zesty cheer,
Whispers of fun linger near.
Twirling dance of flavors bright,
Citrus colors paint the night.

Laughing loud, we clink our cups,
Feeling light, we share the ups.
Sour faces turn to smiles,
With every sip, we span the miles.

Fireflies twinkle like our dreams,
Chasing flows like rippling streams.
Joyful moments, bright and sweet,
In citrus sunsets, we find our beat.

With the stars, our laughter plays,
In the twilight's gentle haze.
We'll sip and sing till night is done,
In these vibes, we find our fun.

Golden Elixirs

In a jug so bright and sweet,
Sipping joy, can't be beat.
Straws dance like they're alive,
With each slurp, we all thrive.

A splash of giggles, a twist of lime,
Every gulp feels like summertime.
Grown-ups laugh, kids act bold,
Stories of silliness unfold.

Frogs leap high, the sun winks down,
Sipping bliss in this warm town.
In sticky hands, the magic swirls,
Funny faces, flips, and twirls.

Golden elixirs, pure delight,
Bringing smiles, feeling light.
Every sip, a burst of cheer,
A toast to laughter and no fear.

Sunkissed Moments

Sunshine spills in every glass,
Giggling kids run in a mass.
Sticky fingers, hats askew,
With a straw, they start to chew.

Ice cubes clink as stories flow,
Sunkissed tales, we steal the show.
Lemon joy in epic sips,
Even grandpa does funny flips.

Chasing shadows in the sun,
Everything feels so much fun.
Messy hair and sand between toes,
A snapshot of laughter we chose.

With every glug and every cheer,
We fill our hearts with love sincere.
In this moment, pure and bright,
We find our joy in sunlight.

Pitchers of Paradise

Welcome to our paradise,
Where laughter blooms and joy flies.
A pitcher spills its fruity stream,
Giddy dreams bursting at the seam.

Cup after cup, the fun won't end,
Silly dances, we all blend.
With goofy hats and vibrant ties,
Everyone's laughing 'til sun dry.

Bending straws like funny tricks,
Each sip a reason for silly picks.
Ice cream floats, a wild addition,
To our party's wild mission.

In this haven of delight,
We sip our joys and dance in light.
Pitchers filled with zesty cheer,
Waves of laughter, loud and clear.

Liquid Sunshine

Liquid sunshine in my cup,
Watch it sparkle, watch it sup.
Frogs jump in, they start to croak,
In sips of joy, they play and joke.

Funny faces, spilling fun,
With each pour, we all run.
Twirly straws and silly cheers,
Bubbles burst, igniting peers.

Summer breeze and sunshine rays,
Laughter echoes through the bays.
We sip and swirl, embrace the day,
In this sweetness, we will stay.

Liquid sunshine, friends do meet,
In moments tasty, oh so sweet.
Raise your cup and let all know,
Laughter shines, let joy flow.

Chill of Citrus Dreams

In the shade of a popsicle tree,
Sipping the sun, so wild and free.
Lemons giggle in a sunny play,
Who knew zest could brighten the day?

With straws like swords, we battle the heat,
A splash of giggles in each sunny greet.
Bubbles dance on the rim of our glass,
Moments like these, too sweet to pass.

Riding on laughter, we swerve and swing,
Citrus notes on the breeze take wing.
A twist of mischief with every sip,
In this funny realm, we'll never slip.

So here's to the days with laughter so bright,
Where lemonade dreams make everything right.
We chase the clouds with a lemony cheer,
A flavor of fun that's perfectly clear.

Squeeze of Joy

Racing to chase the ice cream truck,
With cups of sunshine and a little luck.
Popping bubbles from fizzy cups,
Squeezing the day, we can't get enough.

A splash here, a dribble there,
Sticky hands and messy hair.
We giggle loud, so nothing's amiss,
In our own world, we brew the bliss.

With every pour and every twist,
We stir up fun that can't be missed.
Pinks and yellows in a funny swirl,
Our citrus kingdom makes us twirl.

So raise a toast to silly days,
When laughter's the theme in playful ways.
In every cup, there's joy galore,
Squeezed from life, we always want more.

Vibrant Melodies

A symphony played in a fruit stand,
With chords of citrus, sweet and grand.
Twisting flavors in a waltzing spree,
   Each sip a note in our melody.

Lemons sing in a quirky duet,
With bursts of giggles—we won't forget.
In sunny harmony, we skip and sway,
   Capturing laughter in every spray.

With friends like these, time hits replay,
As fizzy tunes whisk our cares away.
So here's to laughter, bright and bold,
In vibrant rhythms, the tales unfold.

We dance with joy, our spirits soar,
Crafting memories worth to explore.
Let's pop the cork, release the cheer,
In this fruity sonnet, we hold so dear.

Youthful Squeeze

With muddy feet and sun-kissed cheeks,
We wander where the lemonade speaks.
Squeezed dreams flow like sunny streams,
In a world of giggles, not just extremes.

Glasses clink with a jolly cheer,
Creating stories that we hold near.
Wobbling tables with playful tunes,
Summer days beneath the cartoons.

With pouches full of juicy delight,
We stargaze with straws in the night.
Chilling time with a fruity embrace,
Life's a dance; let's set the pace.

Our youthful squeeze, so fresh and spry,
We'll sip on joy until the sun's shy.
In every moment, we find our ray,
Building laughter in a breezy ballet.

Sun-Dappled Delights

In bright sunlight, we toast with cheer,
Sipping joy, with friends so dear.
Sticky fingers, laughter spills,
Chasing dreams on grassy hills.

The bees buzz loud, a sweet parade,
Crafting stories that won't fade.
With every splash, the giggles bloom,
Our worries melt like ice in June.

A pitcher waits, the fun won't cease,
Flavor dances, bringing peace.
We chuckle loud, the sun's our stage,
In this moment, we're all the rage.

With every sip, a memory sweet,
Summer's heat, a tasty treat.
Life's zany joy, we celebrate,
In sun-dappled bliss, we gravitate.

Zesty Journeys

On the road, we bounce and sway,
In search of zest, we laugh and play.
Bumpy rides and silly tunes,
Our hearts are light like bright balloons.

Sipping sunshine from a cup,
The world outside just lights us up.
Citrus dreams in swirling skies,
Chasing clouds, oh how time flies!

From city streets to fields so wide,
We find our joy, our playful pride.
With each new taste, we find our way,
Adventure calls, we can't delay!

A twist of fate, a spritz of fun,
Under the rays, we run and run.
With laughter echoing through the air,
Zesty journeys, none can compare.

Sparkling Memories

With fizzy drinks and cheers around,
Creating moments that astound.
Each bubble bursts like dreams in flight,
Shining brightly in the night.

Friends gather close for tales so loud,
Laughter rises, we're so proud.
Splashing fun with every sip,
Joyful hearts in every trip.

Sweet and tangy, memories blend,
In this moment, we transcend.
Catch the glow of summer's gleam,
Life's a spark in the whimsy stream.

Like stars that twinkle in the dark,
These sparkling times leave a mark.
Toast to joy and giggles bright,
In our hearts, it feels so right.

Sweet Rituals

With sticky hands and grins so wide,
We gather close, arms open wide.
A pitcher full of sunny smiles,
Let's sip and savor for a while.

Each tasting brings a silly cheer,
The sweetness tickles, draws us near.
Under shade, we share our dreams,
In laughter's flow, our spirit beams.

The clinks of cups, a sacred art,
In every sip, we play our part.
With silly games and tongues so sweet,
These rituals, a joyful treat.

So come, dear friends, let's find our way,
To relish cloudy, breezy days.
With every moment, together we rise,
In the sweetness of life, we recognize.

Simple Pleasures in a Glass

When life hands you lemons, don't pout,
Just squeeze and mix, let laughter out.
Add ice, a splash, and stir with glee,
Sip slow, my friend, it's pure jubilee.

With every drop, a giggle bursts,
Sweet and tangy, quenching thirsts.
Beats the drudgery, it's quite clear,
A fizzy laugh, let out a cheer!

So gather 'round, share this delight,
In sunshine beams, feel spirits light.
A toast to joy, the moments sway,
In every glass, a fun-filled day!

Simple sips, the heart's embrace,
Find treasures in this zesty space.
For in these flavors, side by side,
Are memories made, with joy and pride.

Limoncello Wishes

Wishes take flight on rosy wings,
With every sip, a joy that sings.
Sunshine dances in every round,
Glassy smiles, laughter unbound.

A clink of glasses, the mood gets bright,
In this fizzy realm, all feels right.
Pucker and giggle, a playful sting,
With each delight, the heart takes wing.

Lively banter, a cheerful race,
We swap our tales, we find our place.
Zesty dreams whirl like a dance,
In this concoction, we take a chance!

So lift your glass, let wishes soar,
In the world of tang, we beg for more.
With laughter bubbling, we seize the day,
In limoncello's glee, we play!

Sunshine in a Pitcher

A pitcher full of cheerful light,
Pour out the rays, banish the night.
Sprinkled sweetness, a lemony flair,
With giddy sips, we float in air.

Gather your pals, let joy abound,
In this concoction, fun is found.
Chilled to perfection, a summer breeze,
With laughter and zest, we do as we please.

Each sip a giggle, each gulp a cheer,
In this sun-drenched world, bring everyone near!
The frosty rim's a playful tease,
As we bask in laughter, hearts at ease.

With fruity chunks and minty twist,
A perfect blend, we can't resist.
In every drop, a smile conveyed,
With sunshine in a pitcher, we wade!

The Essence of Cheer

In a jar of sunshine, the essence flows,
Bright as the smile that always grows.
Bubbles tease, the giggles start,
A toast to joy, it warms the heart.

Sipping slowly, we hold the glass,
For every laugh, let worries pass.
Fizzy laughter fills the air,
In this sweet moment, we have no care.

Flavorful fun in every drop,
Watch as grumpiness takes a hop.
With fruity gems floating around,
We lose ourselves in joy profound.

Leave your problems at the door,
With every sip, we crave for more.
So swirl your drink, let out a cheer,
In the essence of cheer, let's disappear!

Fresh Squeezes of Joy

On a bright day, we frolic around,
With citrus smiles, joy is found.
Squeezing lemons, a laughter spree,
Who knew a fruit could set us free?

We dance in puddles, sticky and sweet,
Sugar pours in, a tasty treat.
Friends join in, it's a zesty game,
Every splash feels like a new fame.

Mustaches of syrup, we laugh and play,
Refreshing giggles on this sunlit day.
With each gulp, our worries fade,
Living for moments that joy has made.

A Glass Full of Sunshine

Sunshine's bright, and so is our drink,
Sip it slow, let the good times sync.
With every gulp, we chase the grays,
Filling our hearts in the funniest ways.

Wobbly chairs and silly straws,
Lemon zingers, get ready for applause!
Squeezed laughter rings through the air,
Oh, what fun, without a care!

Bouncing on lawns, we take a leap,
In this sweet cup, we dive so deep.
With ice cubes clinking, the wild fun flows,
Let's toast to sunshine that always glows.

Spicy Days and Cool Nights

Spicy days with laughter and cheer,
Chasing the breeze, the fun draws near.
Nightfall whispers, let's cool it down,
Dancing shadows, we flip and frown.

Cayenne and sugar, what a pair!
Heat and chill, oh, we're quite the flair.
Lemon slices smile in our cups,
Bringing joy with each silly hiccup.

Fireflies twinkle in the moonlight glow,
Our giggles dance fast, putting on a show.
Every sip a memory, vivid and bright,
We toast to laughter all through the night.

Sunshine and Sugar

Up in the sky, the sun beams wide,
With a splash of sugar, we can't abide.
Syrups and giggles, a cocktail we make,
Each drop a smile, what a tasty quake!

With friends all around, we share the fun,
Chasing down happiness, everyone.
In sticky afternoons, we climb real high,
Sugar rush fueled by the bright blue sky.

Lemons in hand, we tackle the day,
Laughter bubbles like the drinks we play.
With each refreshing sip we find,
A world of joy, forever intertwined.

Refreshing Bliss

In the sun, we grin and play,
With yellow drinks on a bright display.
Sipping laughter, tart and sweet,
Summer's joy, a tasty treat.

Ice cubes dance in cups of cheer,
Popping colors, bright and clear.
Giggles mix with citrus cheer,
As friends gather, summer near.

Sticky fingers, brightened cheeks,
Funny faces, laughter peaks.
A splash of fun in every sip,
With each warm day, we take a trip.

Glasses clink, the sun's ablaze,
In moments sweet, we lose our ways.
Refreshing bliss, oh what a play,
In sunny sips, we love to stay.

The Zest of Summer

A twist of fruit, a sip of fun,
Beneath the shining, scorching sun.
Laughter bubbles, joy on tap,
In a big cup, we take a nap.

Squeezing smiles with every pour,
A zesty dance, who could want more?
Friends in line for summer's fare,
With funny hats and messy hair.

Tart and sweet in every blend,
This sunny brew we all commend.
Straws like rockets, drinks take flight,
We sip and cheers to night's delight!

With sticky fingers, tales unfold,
Of citrus laughter, bright and bold.
The zest of summer, sweetly done,
In every glass, our hearts have won.

Tangy Dreams

Citrus clouds float up so high,
With silly grins, we reach the sky.
A tangy twist, a playful sigh,
In summer's dance, we all comply.

Sipping dreams of lemon trees,
Feeling light, just like a breeze.
Laughter spritzing, joy won't cease,
In funny moments, we find peace.

A splash of fun, a twist so bright,
Under sunbeams, we feel light.
Each sip brings giggles, pure delight,
In colorful cups, our spirits ignite.

Tangy dreams in games we play,
As sprightly friends come out to stay.
With every clink, we toast to glee,
In this sweet world, we're wild and free.

Delicate Drops of Joy

Morning sun with a citrus hue,
In playful glasses, laughter grew.
Delicate drops, a merry cheer,
Sipping memories of summer near.

Giggling kids on the front lawn,
Chasing flavors 'til the dawn.
A twist of tart, a dash of sweet,
Joy pours out, can't be beat!

Barefoot fun on warm, soft grass,
Funny moments just come to pass.
With sticky hands and brightened eyes,
Each sip a gift, a sweet surprise.

Delicate drops, oh what a game,
In every cup, we share the same.
A summer toast, a friendly spark,
In sunny bliss, we leave our mark.

Sours and Hues

A twist of yellow, a splash of green,
Mismatched socks and a cheeky scene.
Smiles are bubbling, laughter's the key,
Sip on the sunshine, come dance with me.

The birds are chirping a silly tune,
Wobbling like jelly, we'll float to the moon.
Pucker your lips, it's a juicy affair,
With sprinkles of happiness swirling in air.

Giggling gnomes on the garden gate,
Daring each other, oh isn't it great?
We'll mix up the chaos with sugar and zest,
Each sip a giggle, we savor the best.

So gather your friends, let's toast to the sun,
With cups overflowing, we're having such fun.
In this fruity frenzy, oh what a craze,
Let's drink to the joys of our sours and hues!

Sweet Simplicity

In a tiny glass, a treasure we find,
A dash of sunshine, it's simply divine.
With giggles like bubbles, life's never a bore,
Sweet sips of laughter, who could want more?

A twist of a straw, and a playful grin,
Every sip tells a story, let the fun begin!
Knock-knock jokes float on the air so light,
Sprinkling joy like a starry night.

Sticky fingers wave, and the day rolls along,
In our world of sweetness, we all belong.
Simplicity sings in this zest-filled delight,
As we toast to the silly, the smiles shining bright.

So lift up your glass, let's cheer with delight,
To sweetness and laughter that takes flight.
With every delicious chuckle we chase,
Let's savor the moments, the smiles we embrace.

Sunshine Sips

A cup of sunshine served with a grin,
We're spinning in circles, it's chaos within.
Sipping the bright, with a twist on the side,
In this carnival moment, let's enjoy the ride.

Juggling our cups, oh what a fresh mess,
Drips down our elbows, but who wants to stress?
Citrus giggles and happy, loud shrieks,
Flavors of summer, in fun little peaks.

We'll splash in the puddles of giggly delight,
With sticky sweet fingers reaching for height.
A parade of colors dances on our lips,
As we gather the smiles, in sunshine sips.

So let's clink our glasses, make joyful toasts,
With laughter our anthem, come celebrate, folks!
In each sunny gulp, let's raise our cheer,
To the zany adventures that bring us here.

Sweet Citrus Serenade

A melody dances on citrusy air,
With laughter that bubbles, it's fun everywhere.
The jingle of ice clinks, a sweet serenade,
In our quirky world, let's boldly parade.

Little critters giggle in the warm afternoon,
As we twirl with flavors like a happy cartoon.
Each sip a giggle, a burst full of cheer,
As we sing and we swirl, the joy is near.

With sassy umbrellas and cups full of glee,
We're splattering sunshine, just you wait and see.
In this joyous orchard, the fun never fades,
With sweet citrus whispers orchestrating ballets.

So join in the chorus of flavors and laughs,
With zesty delight that forever outlasts.
In the mix of this joy, let's create our tune,
A sweet summer's song beneath the bright moon!

Tangy Reflections

Fuzzy sunburns and sticky hands,
A pitcher waits, oh what a plan.
With citrus smiles and giggles loud,
We're tasting joys, feeling quite proud.

Sipping sweet till our cheeks go red,
A splash of joy, our worries fled.
We pucker up, just like the fruit,
In this funny tale, our laughter's root.

When life gives us a zesty squeeze,
We turn frowns into lemonade tease.
A cheerful twist, a fruity punch,
Who knew such fun could come from lunch?

With laughter bubbling, in the sun's embrace,
Our goofy dances, a silly race.
So let's blend joy, both tart and sweet,
Today's a treat, oh what a feat!

Moments of Tartness

When life gets sour, we take a sip,
A dash of giggles, a little trip.
Sunshine shines on our frosty glasses,
As we swap stories, time truly passes.

Sticky fingers grab the fun,
In juicy games, we laugh and run.
Tartness fills the air so bright,
Sweet humor blends, oh what a sight!

We squirt the juice, with playful glee,
A cheeky smile, just you and me.
With every gulp, we feel that zing,
In this moment, joy's the favorite fling.

A hint of citrus, a burst of cheer,
Creating memories we hold so dear.
These moments shared, both sweet and wild,
Life's a blast, let happiness be our child!

Spritz of Laughter

Zingy sparks in the summer sun,
A fizzy drink, now let's have fun.
With every sip, a funny face,
Awkward flavors, but full of grace.

Twirling straws and shouts of glee,
Lemon zest, oh woe is me!
A splash on shirts, a giggling mess,
In joyful chaos, we feel so blessed.

Tickling taste buds, we can't resist,
Each sip a chuckle, a fruity twist.
Bring on the laughter, bring on the cheer,
In this spritz of life, let's persevere.

So pour it high and enjoy each day,
In this silly game, we're here to stay.
With wit as sharp as a citrus slice,
We laugh and sip, oh how nice!

Bright Days Ahead

Dancing shadows on the grassy floor,
A splash of fun, who could ask for more?
Sweet scents of summer fill the space,
With cheeky smiles, we embrace the chase.

The sun may set, but we stay awake,
In our fruity world, mistakes we shake.
A mix of joy in every cup,
We tip it back and laugh it up.

With every drop, we seize the day,
Our laughter bounces, come what may.
The future glimmers, like lemonade,
Bright moments unfold, never to fade.

So here's to days both sweet and bright,
With zestful laughter, we take flight.
In this journey, let's raise a cheer,
To the funny memories, we hold dear!

Savoring Sunlit Mornings

The sun arrives, a zesty cheer,
Bright rays bounce off my glass so clear.
Sipping slow, with giggles galore,
I dance like nobody's keeping score.

The garden blooms with vibrant hues,
Tickling my toes in sunshine shoes.
Butterflies waltz, a cheerful sight,
Each sip is joy, pure and light.

With friends, we share our silly tales,
As laughter bubbles, the joy never fails.
The clock ticks slow, a day well spent,
In golden sips, our hearts consent.

A splash of fun in every drop,
Radiant smiles that never stop.
As sun sets down, a gentle sway,
Mark this moment, come what may.

Frosty Reverie

A summer's drink in frosty glass,
Chilly breeze, while moments pass.
I take a sip, a shocking chill,
My face reacts, what a thrill!

Ice cubes dance, a merry jive,
In this cool cup, I'm so alive.
Twists and turns of flavor bright,
Delightful sip, what a sight!

Join the fun, let laughter ring,
As we chase summer's joyful fling.
The world a blur outside our window,
In frosty dreams, we laugh and grow.

Voices mix in crazy cheer,
Every clink a memory dear.
The joy expands, we freeze the day,
In frosty reveries, we play.

Laughter and Lemons

Squeezed too tight, the citrus mocks,
A face like mine, it surely rocks!
The sour's sweet in playful jest,
Who knew the tart could be the best?

With friends around, the jokes fly high,
As lemon peels, we laugh and sigh.
The pucker faces, oh what a treat,
In this citrus world, we can't be beat.

A dash of sugar, a twist of fate,
Our giggles echo, it's never late.
The zest of life in every cup,
To keep our spirits bubble up!

So hold your glass, let spirits soar,
In laughter's flow, who could ask for more?
A playful sip, a silly cheer,
In citrus fun, we find our gear.

Cherry Blossom Breeze

In breezy whispers, petals play,
Cherry blossoms dance, hooray!
The sweetness swirls on every path,
As giggles rise, we share a laugh.

A swirl of pink, a hint of cheer,
With every sip, joy draws near.
Tickled pink in evening light,
Life's simple moments feel so right.

The cup is full, the spirits bright,
Laughter sparkles in twilight.
With cherry whispers in the air,
We sip and savor without a care.

As blossoms fall like confetti dress,
Our hearts, our laughter, we'll never suppress.
In this cherry breeze, we sway and spin,
In life's sweet game, together we win.

Sunlit Revelry

In the yard with cups in hand,
Laughter echoes, oh so grand.
Sipping drinks that shine so bright,
Silly faces, pure delight.

Racing over grass so green,
Chasing bubbles, a joyful scene.
Sprite and giggles fill the air,
Sunshine dances without a care.

With sticky fingers, we all yell,
'Best day ever!' as we dwell.
A splash of laughter, a twist of fun,
Chasing rainbows, we all run.

So here's to days of sweet surprise,
With sunshine swirling in our eyes.
Holding hands, we take a bow,
For summer's joy is here right now.

Nectar of the Season

Mugs and pitchers lined up wide,
Sugary nectar, joy in stride.
Sipping slow, a citrus cheer,
Every drop brings smiles near.

Giggles burst like bubbles pop,
Wobbling dance moves, oh, don't stop!
Straws like pirates, our battle cry,
Swirling waves as clouds roll by.

Mustard stains on favorite shirts,
Splatters of fun, and feeble flirts.
Everyone's got their silly hat,
Watching leaves flutter, imagining that.

Here's to fun in sunny glades,
Under the trees where childhood wades.
A toast to laughter, joy, and play,
In perfect harmony, we'll stay.

Golden Harvest

Beneath the sun, we gather round,
With golden cups where joy is found.
Freshly squeezed with love and grace,
Faces glowing, smiles on every face.

The table decked with treats galore,
Dancing kids run through the door.
Sticky fingers, laughter loud,
This sunny day's our joyful crowd.

We stomp our feet, a silly jig,
Feeling bold, we dance, we dig.
In every sip, a zest for life,
Flavors burst, dispelling strife.

So let the sun keep shining bright,
As we indulge in sweet delight.
Friends and fun, as sweet as pie,
Together, we'll reach for the sky.

The Taste of Summer Dreams

In the shade, we sip and smile,
Refreshing smiles that stretch a mile.
Mellow moments, laughter spills,
Each gulp brings joy, and time stands still.

With goofy straws, and messy hands,
We make silly, crazy plans.
Stomping on grass, a dance we play,
In this dreamy realm, we sway.

Dreams of flavors, bright and sweet,
Follow the giggles, move your feet.
A pinch of this and a splash right there,
Our concoctions send giggles in the air.

A summer bliss that's hard to hide,
With joy and fun walking beside.
Chasing whispers of light and cheer,
Forever held in this moment dear.

Whispers of the Orchard

In the orchard where the lemons grow,
Kids are laughing, putting on a show.
Sticky fingers from the little treats,
Chasing shadows with their tiny feet.

Sun-kissed cheeks and giggles fly,
Lemonade stands, oh my oh my!
Silly faces, a painted grin,
Fruit fights start, let the games begin!

A splash of juice, a silly cheer,
Citrus smiles from ear to ear.
Pitched tents for an afternoon rest,
Nature's sweetness is simply the best.

Whispers of laughter blend with the breeze,
Nature's candy, as sweet as you please.
In the orchard, life feels so bright,
Every sip brings pure delight.

Cozy Sips

Gather 'round for a playful mix,
Sipping warmth with our lemon tricks.
Tangy zest in every drop,
A clumsy sip, and off we hop!

Messy straws and unwieldy cups,
Chasing laughter, filling up our ups.
Fuzzy bees dance in the sun,
Swatting them away—what silly fun!

Chill the pitcher, a citrus wave,
Slurp it down, not one to save!
With every giggle and clatter loud,
We toast to summer; we're oh so proud!

Fingers sticky, a funny scene,
And under the tree, we share our dream.
Sipping sunshine, hearts in a whirl,
Cozy times as the laughter unfurls.

Tasting Summer's Kiss

Bright yellow globes hang in the sun,
We craft our drinks, oh what fun!
Stiring giggles in the fragrant air,
Sipping happiness, without a care.

A twist of sugar, a dash of cheer,
Every drop whispers, summer is here!
Round the table, stories we trade,
With a fruity splash, our troubles fade.

Bright straw hats dance in the breeze,
With every sip, we aim to please.
Raspberry swirls or mint leaves spry,
Mix a little chaos, let laughter fly!

What's better than sweet, tangy bliss?
Catching moments in a fizzy kiss.
We sip and smile, as rays warmly glow,
Toasting the sun, letting joy overflow.

A Dance in the Orchard

Underneath the lemon trees,
We stomp and twirl with quirky ease.
Feet in rhythm, hearts beat fast,
A whirling dance, oh what a blast!

Sunlight dapples with golden hues,
Fruits and laughter, our playful muse.
Jumping high as the branches sway,
In this sweet grove, let's dance away!

Stick your tongue out for a sip,
With messy hair, we bravely skip.
A symphony of giggles and zest,
In this orchard; we feel so blessed.

So let's keep spinning until we drop,
And toast to laughter, we can't stop!
For in this warmth, friendship does rise,
Under lemon trees, we touch the skies.

www.ingramcontent.com/pod-product-compliance
Lightning Source LLC
Chambersburg PA
CBHW060111230426
43661CB00003B/149